Old Jack's Ghost Stories from Japan

I Talk You Talk Press

CONTENTS

ACKNOWLEDGMENTS

With sincere thanks to Colin Dixon who collected and recorded the stories contained in this volume. Without his contribution this book would not have been possible.

MESSAGE FROM OLD JACK

Hello, and welcome to my book of Japanese ghost stories. A few years ago, I visited Ireland to do some research for my book *Old Jack's Ghost Stories from Ireland*. One evening, I was sitting in the hotel bar, when I met Mr Yamada, a Japanese tourist. He was sitting at the table next to mine. We started talking. Mr Yamada had travelled to Ireland for an interesting reason. He wanted to visit the childhood home of the writer Lafcadio Hearn.

Lafcadio Hearn was born in 1850 and died in 1904. He travelled to Japan, and lived in Matsue, Mr Yamada's hometown, for about a year. There, he married the daughter of a samurai. They had four children, and Lafcadio spent the rest of his life in Japan.

I was interested to hear Mr Yamada's story about Lafcadio Hearn, but I was even more interested when he told me that Lafcadio Hearn researched and collected Japanese ghost stories! Mr Yamada and I talked for a long time. He told me about his hometown. He said, "Lafcadio Hearn's house is still there. Now, it is a popular tourist spot. You should visit Matsue. You can stay with me! I will tell you Hearn's ghost stories, and take you sightseeing!"

Mr Yamada and I exchanged addresses, and we wrote to each other regularly. Then, last year, in the autumn, when the leaves were turning red and orange, I decided to visit Mr Yamada and learn about Japanese ghosts.

So, come and join me on my great adventure in the wonderful country of Japan and enjoy the mysterious world of Lafcadio Hearn's Japanese ghost stories.

1. A MOTHER'S LOVE

Place: Daio-ji Temple, Matsue City, Shimane Prefecture

I arrived in Matsue in the early afternoon. Mr Yamada and his wife were waiting for me. We shook hands.

"It's good to see you again Old Jack san! Welcome to my hometown!" said Mr Yamada.

"It's wonderful to see you too!" I said.

"It's nice to meet you," said Mrs Yamada.

"It's nice to meet you too, Mrs Yamada," I said.

"What should I call you?" she asked.

"Call me Old Jack," I said. "Everybody calls me Old Jack."

They took me to their home, a beautiful traditional Japanese house, near Matsue Castle.

We went into the house and they took me to my room. Mr Yamada opened the sliding paper doors, and said, "Is this room OK for you, Old Jack san?"

"Oh yes, it's wonderful!" I said. It had beautiful tatami mats, and sliding paper blinds, called shoji, on the windows. It had a view of the Yamada's traditional garden. It was very different from my house in England. It was charming, and very peaceful.

Maybe Lafcadio Hearn felt like this when he first came here, I thought.

I was tired after my long trip, so I had a rest for a few hours. Then, Mr Yamada said to me, "Let's go for a walk. I'll take you to a place with an interesting story."

We walked through the quiet, narrow streets to a place called Nakabara-machi.

"Lafcadio Hearn told an interesting story about this area," said Mr Yamada.

"A ghost story?" I asked.

Mr Yamada smiled. "Yes. A long time ago, there was a small sweet shop here. The shop sold a kind of sweet syrup, called mizu-ame. Mothers gave it to children when there was little milk. One night, just before the shop closed, a woman entered the shop. The shop owner looked at her. She was very thin and pale, and she looked very tired.

"The shop owner thought, *I've never seen her before. She looks sick and tired. Is she OK?*

"The woman bought a small amount of mizu-ame, and left the shop."

"Did she say anything to the shop owner?" I asked.

"No, she didn't. She came back the next night, and the night after that. After a few nights, the shop owner started to worry because the woman looked so sick. So, he decided to follow her."

We stopped walking, and stood outside a temple called Daio-ji. It was my first time to see a Japanese temple, so I took some photographs.

"So, did he follow the woman?" I asked.

"Yes, he did."

"Where did she go?" I asked.

"She came here," said Mr Yamada. "The shop owner followed her to the temple gate and stopped. He was very frightened, so he did not enter the temple."

"Why? The woman lived at the temple. That's not frightening, is it?" I asked.

Mr Yamada smiled. "Well yes, but no…hmm…follow me."

We walked through the temple gate and into a graveyard.

"You see, this is a graveyard."

I looked around. It seemed peaceful in the late afternoon sun.

"The next night, the shop owner decided to follow the woman again. But this time, he asked his friends to go with him. They followed her into this graveyard. When she arrived at a tomb, she disappeared!"

"Disappeared? Where did she go?" I asked.

"Well, the shop owner and his friends heard a strange noise from one of the tombs. It sounded like a baby crying. They were very frightened, but they lifted up the tombstone and they saw the body of the woman. She was dead. But next to her, there was a child. The child was alive. And next to the child, there was a cup of mizu-ame."

"Oh!" I said. I was shocked.

"The ghost of the dead mother bought the mizu-ame every night, to feed her child."

We stood quietly, looking at the graves. Then Mr Yamada smiled.

"Of course, Old Jack san, we don't know if this story is true or not. But, I like to think it is true."

I agreed with Mr Yamada. I hoped it was a true story. Thanks to the love of the dead mother for her child, the young child was found and saved.

2. THE LAUGHING SAMURAI

Place: Near Fumon-in Temple, Matsue City, Shimane Prefecture

That night, Mrs Yamada served some wonderful sushi. After dinner, we sat in the living room. Mr Yamada said, "I know you like whisky Old Jack san. Have you ever tried Japanese whisky?"

"No, I haven't! But I'd like to try it!" I said.

Mr Yamada opened a bottle and poured some into a glass for me. I tried it.

"This is excellent! It's very smooth!" I said.

"So, Old Jack san, did you enjoy your visit to Daio-ji today?" asked Mrs Yamada.

"Oh yes, I did," I said. "I enjoyed the ghost story about the mother and her child."

"There's a ghost story about a father and his child too," said Mrs Yamada.

"Is there? Here? In Matsue?" I asked.

"Yes, Lafcadio Hearn put it in his book," said Mrs Yamada.

"Oh, yes," said Mr Yamada. "I'll take you to the place tomorrow."

The next day was warm and sunny. We walked up past Matsue Castle, and along a river. I took many photographs. There are so many rivers and bridges in Matsue. It seems to be a city built on water. I was enjoying the walk, when Mr Yamada stopped suddenly.

"This is Fumon-in Temple," he said. "A long time ago, Old Jack san, there was a bridge here. It was called The Bridge of the Washing of Peas."

"Washing of peas?" I asked. "That's a strange name for a bridge! Why was it called that?"

"Well, many years ago, people often saw the ghost of a woman under the bridge. The ghost was washing peas," said Mr Yamada. "There is a purple flower in Japan, called kaki-tsubata. There is an old song about this flower. People said that the ghost didn't like this song. If she heard a person singing the song, she would hurt them!"

"Why?" I asked.

"No one knows. But everyone believed the story, so no one sang the song near the bridge."

"That's interesting," I said.

"Oh, I haven't finished," said Mr Yamada. "One night, a samurai heard the story about the song. This samurai was not afraid of anything. 'Is it true?' he asked. 'Let's see!' He walked through the quiet streets and stood on the bridge. Then, very loudly, he began to sing the flower song. He stopped and looked around. Then, he started to laugh. 'Ha ha ha! See! Nothing happened! Nothing happened!'"

"That samurai was either very strong, or very foolish," I said.

Mr Yamada nodded his head. "The samurai started to walk home. When he was near his house, he saw a very tall, beautiful woman. *Who is she?* he thought. *I've never seen her before.* As he got closer to the woman, she bowed her head and gave him a beautiful box. It was a box for keeping letters in. He was very surprised. 'Thank you,' he said. The woman looked at him. 'Do not thank me. I am only a servant. The gift is from my mistress', she said. Then, she disappeared."

I started to feel cold.

Mr Yamada continued. "The samurai opened the box. 'What?' he shouted. 'No!' Inside the box, there was the head of a young child. He ran into his house, and there, he found the dead body of his young son. The samurai had stood on the bridge, singing the flower song. Then, he had laughed. It seems the ghost of the woman who washed peas wanted revenge."

We stood in silence for a while. It was interesting. In the first story, the love of a ghost had saved a child, but in this story, the attitude of a father, and an angry ghost, had killed a child.

"What would you like to do now Old Jack san? Lafcadio Hearn's old house is near here. We can go inside it," said Mr Yamada.

6

"Can we have something to drink first?" I asked.

"Yes, of course. There is a café near here. Would you like tea?"

After hearing that story, I wanted something a little stronger than tea, but it was still morning. I was sure Mr Yamada didn't want to drink whisky so early.

"Yes, tea is fine," I said.

3. THE BLIND MAN WHO COULD SEE

Place: Akama-jingu Shrine, Shimonoseki City, Yamaguchi Prefecture

For our next story, we leave the city of Matsue and travel to the city of Shimonoseki in Yamaguchi Prefecture.

Mr Yamada's friend, Mr Nakamura, had invited us to stay at his house for a few days. One fine morning, Mr Yamada and I took the train from Matsue to Okayama, and then took the bullet train, or shinkansen, to Shimonoseki. It was exciting to ride such a fast train! Mr Nakamura was waiting for us at the station.

It was a long trip, and I was very tired. We went to a restaurant and I enjoyed a bowl of delicious noodles. After that, we went to Mr Nakamura's house. He lives alone in a big house in a quiet area of the city. After a few glasses of local sake, I was ready to go to bed. I slept very well.

The next morning, while we were having breakfast, Mr Nakamura said, "Yamada san told me you like ghost stories."

"Oh yes, I do. Very much," I said. "I'm enjoying learning about Lafcadio Hearn's ghost stories."

"Well, we have a surprise for you, Old Jack san. We are going to take you to the place of Lafcadio Hearn's most famous ghost story!" said Mr Nakamura.

"Oh, excellent!" I said. "Thank you!"

"I arranged with Nakamura san to bring you to Shimonoseki as a surprise. We are going to tell you the story of Hoichi the Earless," said Mr Yamada.

"Hoichi the Earless? This sounds interesting!" I said. "Are we going after breakfast?"

Mr Yamada and Mr Nakamura looked at each other and smiled.

"No, we are going at night. When it is dark," said Mr Nakamura.

During the day, I enjoyed shopping, and I went to a museum. I was looking forward to the night time very much.

After dinner, at around nine pm, we got into Mr Nakamura's car and drove along the sea road. Mr Nakamura parked the car and we got out. We walked to the water. The wind was strong.

Across the water, we could see many lights.

"What is that land over there?" I asked. "Is it an island?"

"That is Kyushu. Maybe you know it. It has famous cities, such as Nagasaki and Fukuoka. That bridge over there links this main island, Honshu, with Kyushu," said Mr Nakamura. "This area is Dan-no-ura. It is a very famous place. A long time ago, there were many battles between the two great families, the Heike and the Genji."

"Oh! I've heard of them. They are very famous, aren't they?" I said.

"Yes, they are. Well, there were many battles here, and the Heike family was completely destroyed. Their women and children were killed too.

"For many centuries, at night, people saw strange, ghostly lights around here. They also heard strange sounds, like people fighting, but the sea was empty."

"Sometimes ships passed here. The sailors on the ships often had strange experiences. They saw the ghosts of Heike soldiers. The ghosts were trying to get out of the water, and climb on the ships," said Mr Yamada.

I looked out at the dark water. It was a warm, autumn night, but I suddenly felt very cold.

"At that time, people said, 'The dead soldiers and their families cannot rest. We have to do something for them.' So, they built a Buddhist temple called Amida-ji here."

"Where?" I asked.

Mr Nakamura pointed behind us. "Over there. Later, it became a shrine. Now, it is Akama-jingu Shrine."

"Can we go and see it?" I asked.

"Not tonight. We will go tomorrow morning when it is open," said Mr Nakamura. "They also built a graveyard for the spirits of the dead people. The temple held Buddhist ceremonies, and people prayed for the Heike family. After that, people didn't see so many strange lights in the water, or hear so many strange things."

"So everything was fine," I said. "But this morning, you said there was a story about a man with no ears. Who was that?"

"Yes, we are going to tell you the story of Hoichi the Earless," said Mr Yamada. "Shall we walk a little?"

We started to walk along the sea road.

"A few hundred years ago, a blind biwa player lived in this area," said Mr Nakamura.

"What is a biwa?" I asked.

"It is a Japanese musical instrument," said Mr Nakamura. "A kind of lute. The blind man was called Hoichi. He was an excellent biwa player. He played and sang songs about the stories and legends of this area. His best songs were about the battle between the Heike and the Genji. When he sang about that, even big men cried!

"Hoichi was very poor, so he was very pleased when the priest at Amida-ji invited him to live in the temple. He didn't have to pay any money for rent, and he didn't have to pay for food. He only had to play and sing for the priest, because the priest loved Hoichi's music.

"One night, the priest had to go out on business. It was a warm night, so Hoichi sat on the platform outside his room and practiced his biwa in the open air.

"Just after midnight, he heard footsteps. *Ah, it is the priest. He has come back,* thought Hoichi. The footsteps crossed the garden and stopped in front him. *Oh, no. It's not the priest,* he thought. *Who is it?*

"A strong voice said, 'Hoichi! Do not be afraid! My lord is staying near here. He sent me to find you. My lord visited the scene of the battle of Dan-no-ura today, and he wants you to sing the story of the battle for him.'

"Hoichi agreed to go and play for the man's lord. Hoichi couldn't see, so the man took Hoichi's hand and led him across the garden and across the town. Hoichi could hear the sound of the man's armour. *He must be a samurai!* he thought. Soon, they stopped.

"'Open the gate!' shouted the man. Hoichi was very surprised. *We are at a gate,* he thought. *Which gate?*

"The gate opened and they went inside. Hoichi could hear many voices. They sounded like servant's voices. *This lord must be very important,* he thought. *This building must be a very big palace.*

"A woman took his hand, and led him to a cushion. He knelt on the cushion, and the woman told him to play the biwa and sing songs about the battle. Everyone in the room was very quiet. They listened very carefully to Hoichi. But then, when Hoichi sang the part about the women and children dying in the battle, many people started to cry. When Hoichi finished, the woman said, 'Hoichi, my lord was very pleased with your performance. He will stay in this area for six nights. He wants you to come back every night while he is here. But, you must not tell anyone about this. Now, you can go back to the temple. We will see you tomorrow night.'

"The samurai took Hoichi back to the temple. The next night, Hoichi visited the lord again. No one at the temple noticed that he wasn't in his room. But on the third night, while Hoichi was performing for the lord, the priest noticed Hoichi was not at the temple. *Where is Hoichi?* he thought. *Why did he go out so late at night? He cannot see! It is dangerous for him to go out alone at night!*

"When Hoichi returned, the priest said, 'Hoichi, where have you been?' Hoichi answered, 'I've been out on private business. Don't worry. I'm not in danger.'

"But the priest was worried, so the next night, he asked his servants to watch Hoichi. The servants sat in another room and waited. They could see Hoichi's room. 'Look!' one of them said. 'Hoichi is standing up! He is going somewhere! Come on, let's follow him!'

"The servants picked up their lanterns and hurried out into the garden to follow Hoichi. It was raining, so they couldn't see very well. 'He walks very fast!' said one of the servants. 'He is blind! How can he walk so fast?'

"Suddenly, the servants stopped. They were in front of the graveyard. They could see Hoichi sitting in front of the graves of the Heike family. He was alone. He was playing his biwa and singing about the battle of Dan-no-ura. And all around him, there were strange lights - the ghostly fires of the dead, floating in the dark night.

"The servants asked him to stop and return to the temple with them, but Hoichi said, 'Do not be so rude! This is the house of a very important and great lord! I will return when I have finished my performance!' The servants thought it was very strange. 'You must return Hoichi! You must return now!' they said.

"Hoichi and the servants returned to the temple. The servants told the priest about Hoichi in the graveyard. The priest was very upset. Hoichi felt bad, so he told the priest about the samurai, and about the lord. The priest said, 'Hoichi! You are in danger! You haven't been going to the house of a lord. You have been going to the graveyard! You have been performing in front of the tombs of the Heike family! They are dead! They are spirits, and now you are in their power! We must protect you!'

"The priest decided to protect Hoichi by writing the text of a Buddhist prayer, Hannya-Shin-Kyo, all over Hoichi's body. The priest and the younger priests used brushes to write the prayer on Hoichi's back, chest, legs, arms, face…everywhere. The priest said, 'I have some business outside the temple tonight. You will be alone. The samurai will come for you again tonight. Do not answer. Stay very quiet.'

"Hoichi was very frightened. That night, he sat on the platform outside his room and waited. Soon, he heard the samurai's footsteps. The samurai said, 'Hoichi! Hoichi!' But Hoichi didn't answer. 'I must find him,' said the samurai. 'Here is his biwa, but where is he?' Then the samurai said, 'I can only see two ears. But there is no mouth, so he can't answer. If I don't take Hoichi to the lord, he will be very angry, so I'll take these ears with me.'

"The samurai pulled Hoichi's ears off! Hoichi was in pain, but he didn't shout or cry. The samurai left the temple. When the priest returned that night he saw blood. 'What?' he said. He ran to Hoichi's room and saw his friend lying in blood, with no ears.

"'Oh no! This is my fault!' said the priest. 'We wrote the prayer on your body, but one of the young priests forgot to write on your ears! I should have checked more carefully! The ghost came for you, but he couldn't see your body. He could only see the parts with no prayers written on them! He could only see your ears!'"

"Oh, that's terrible!" I said. "What happened to Hoichi?"

"The priest found a good doctor, and Hoichi recovered. He became very famous. After that, everyone called him Mimi-Nashi-Hoichi, or Hoichi the Earless," said Mr Nakamura.

"Hoichi the Earless," I said. "I would like to call him Hoichi, the blind man who could see."

Mr Nakamura laughed. "That's an interesting idea."

"It's getting cold," said Mr Yamada. "Let's go back."

We went back to Mr Nakamura's house, and after a few cups of sake, I went to bed. The next morning, we visited Akama-jingu Shrine. It was a beautiful sunny day, and the shrine buildings were wonderful.

We stopped at one small building. Inside, there was a statue of a biwa player.

"This is Hoichi," said Mr Nakamura.

"So Hoichi is still here," I said, looking at the statue. "I wonder if he still plays and sings at night…"

4. THE WOMAN OF THE SNOW

Place: Tokyo area

A few days later, Mr Yamada and I said goodbye to Mr Nakamura, and took the train from Shimonoseki to Kyoto. Before we got on the train, we bought lunch boxes and cans of beer at a shop near the station. While we were eating lunch on the train, Mr Yamada said, "Would you like to hear another ghost story?"

"Of course," I said.

"Well, this story is from Tokyo. But a long time ago, the area was called Musashi Province. The story is about two woodcutters, called Mosaku and Minokichi. Mosaku was an old man, and Minokichi was a young boy, around eighteen years old.

"One day, they were returning home after working very hard in the forest. The forest was on the other side of a river, so every day, they had to cross the river by ferry. When they arrived at the river, they were very surprised.

"'Where is the ferry man?' asked Minokichi. 'His boat is on the other side of the river, and he is not here.'

"'We finished a little later than usual, so he has gone home,' said Mosaku.

"'What are we going to do? How can we get home?' asked Minokichi. Just then, it started to snow heavily.

"'It's a snowstorm,' said Mosaku. 'Come on, let's go to the ferry man's office. It is small, but we will be dry. We can stay in there until morning.'

"So they went to the office and tried to sleep. During the night,

Minokichi woke up. *That's strange,* he thought. *The door is open.* The snow was coming into the office through the open door. 'Ah! What's that?' he said, in surprise.

"In the soft light, he could see a woman in the room. She was dressed in white, and she was very beautiful. Minokichi was very frightened. The woman was bending over Mosaku and breathing cold air on his face. Then, she turned to Minokichi. She said to him, 'You are just a young boy. I will not hurt you now. But you must never tell anyone about this night, or about me. If you tell anyone, I will kill you! Remember this!'"

"Oh, that's terrible!" I said, as I finished my beer. "What happened to Mosaku? Was he OK?"

"Well, the next morning, the ferry man came to the office, and he found Mosaku and Minokichi. Mosaku was dead. Minokichi was very frightened. He said nothing about the woman in the white dress."

Mr Yamada gave me another can of beer. Then, he continued.

"A year passed, and autumn slowly changed into winter. Minokichi was walking home one evening, when he saw a tall girl on the road. She was very beautiful. He said 'Good evening' to her, and they started to talk. 'What's your name?' he asked. 'I'm O-Yuki', she said. 'My parents died recently, and I am alone. I have relatives in Yedo town. I'm going to stay with them, and try to find a job as a servant girl.' Minokichi looked at the girl. She seemed very tired. 'Why don't you take a rest at my house?' he asked.

"So, O-Yuki went to Minokichi's house, and his mother cooked a meal for her. Minokichi's mother liked O-Yuki very much. 'Please stay a little longer,' she said. So O-Yuki stayed. Soon, Minokichi and O-Yuki fell in love, and O-Yuki never went to Yedo. They got married."

"Oh, wonderful! A happy ending!" I said.

Mr Yamada laughed. "I haven't finished yet!" he said. "Five years later, Minokichi's mother died. Before she died, she said, 'O-Yuki is a wonderful wife and daughter-in-law.' Many years passed, and Minokichi and O-Yuki had ten children. But the people in the village thought it was very strange. O-Yuki didn't get older! She had ten children, but she looked very young. One night, after the children had gone to bed, O-Yuki was sewing in the living room. There was only a small lamp, so the room was quite dark. Minokichi was watching her. He said, 'In this soft light, you look like someone I met a long time ago.' O-Yuki looked at him. 'Really? Tell me about her.'

"So Minokichi told her about the night in the ferry man's office. He told her about the woman in the white dress, who brought death to Mosaku. 'In my life, I have seen many women, but only the woman in the white dress is as beautiful as you. I was very frightened. I thought she was the Woman of the Snow...or maybe an Angel of Death...'

"Suddenly, O-Yuki stood up and started to scream. 'It was I! I was the woman in the white dress that night! And I told you not to tell anyone! I said I would kill you if you told anyone!' Minokichi was very frightened. O-Yuki said, 'But we have children, so I will not kill you. Take care of them. If you do not take care of them well, I will return, and you will die!' Then, her body changed into a white mist. The mist rose slowly to the roof, and disappeared. Minokichi watched in silence. Then, he stood up and went to his children's room. He watched them sleeping and made a promise. 'I promise to look after these children until I die.' No one saw O-Yuki again."

Mr Yamada stopped. We looked around. The train was very quiet. Everyone was listening to Mr Yamada's story!

A woman sitting in front of us turned around.

"I enjoyed that story! Thank you!" she said.

Then a young American woman sitting behind us said, "I enjoyed it too. What does the name O-Yuki mean?"

Mr Yamada smiled. "It means snow."

Just then, the train arrived at Kyoto Station "Come on Old Jack san! We get off here!" he said.

When we got off the train, I felt a cold wind. *Autumn is changing to winter,* I thought. *The season of O-Yuki....*

5. SECRETS OF THE HEART

Place: Kyoto area

We spent a few days in Kyoto. It is a wonderful city. There are so many temples to see. We enjoyed walking through the old streets during the day and at night. After a long day sightseeing, we finally went to a restaurant for dinner. It was a traditional Japanese restaurant in a small back street of Kyoto.

"Kyoto is a very old city. There must be many ghost stories here," I said.

"I'm sure there are," said Mr Yamada. "But I only know one of Lafcadio Hearn's ghost stories from here."

"Oh, please tell me," I said.

Mr Yamada put his chopsticks down, and started to speak.

"A long time ago, a rich merchant called Inamuraya Gensuke lived in Tamba Province near Kyoto. He had a daughter, called O-Sono. She was very beautiful and clever, and the merchant was very proud of her. He sent her to a school in Kyoto for a good education. When she returned, she married a friend of her father's family. They had a son, and they were very happy together. But four years after they married, O-Sono became sick, and she died. On the night after the funeral, all the family gathered in the living room of the house. O-Sono's young son was upstairs. Suddenly, he came downstairs and said to everyone, 'Mama has come back! Mama is here! She is in her bedroom! She smiled at me, but she didn't talk to me.'

"A few members of the family went upstairs and looked in the bedroom. They were very shocked to see O-Sono's ghost. The ghost was standing in front of a tansu."

"I'm sorry, but what is a tansu?" I asked.

"It is a chest of drawers. O-Sono kept her kimono and accessories in it," said Mr Yamada. "So, when they saw the ghost, they ran downstairs and talked about it. 'Why did she come back?' they asked each other. Then the mother of O-Sono's husband said, 'I think she came back because she wanted to look at her kimono and accessories. They are very fine things.' Everyone agreed. She said, 'Let's take her kimono and other things to the local temple. Her spirit will rest if we take everything there. She won't come back to this house anymore.' So, they took everything out of the tansu, and took it all to the local temple. But it was no good."

"Why not?" I asked.

"Well, the next night, she came back. The family saw her standing in front of the tansu again. She came back every night after that. Everyone in the family was very frightened. So, the next day, the mother of O-Sono's husband went to the temple to ask the priest for help. The chief priest's name was Daigen Osho. He listened carefully, and then he said, 'She is worried about something. There is something in the tansu.' The woman said, 'No, there is nothing in the tansu. We brought everything here, to the temple. The tansu is empty.' The priest said, 'OK, I will visit the house tonight. I will stay in O-Sono's bedroom and wait for her. But the family must stay away from the bedroom while I am there.'

"That night, the priest stayed in O-Sono's bedroom. Very late at night, O-Sono's ghost came. The priest saw her appear in front of the tansu. She seemed very sad, and she was looking only at the tansu. The priest said a prayer, and then he said, 'O-Sono, I came here to help you. Is there something in the tansu? Would you like me to look for it?' O-Sono nodded her head. So the priest opened all the drawers in the tansu. Every drawer was empty. But then he saw something. There was paper lining the drawers. He lifted up the paper, and he found a letter. He looked at O-Sono. 'Is this letter the problem?' O-Sono turned towards the priest and looked at the letter. 'Shall I burn it for you?' he asked. She nodded. 'I will do it in the morning. I will burn it alone. No one else will see it.' O-Sono smiled, and then disappeared.

"The priest went downstairs and said to the family, 'Do not be frightened. She will not come back again.' And O-Sono never came back."

"What was in the letter?" I asked.

"Well, the priest looked at it before he burned it. It was a love letter from a man in Kyoto. O-Sono had met him when she was a student, before she got married. Only the priest knew the contents of the letter. When he died, the secret died too."

Mr Yamada smiled. "What do you think, Old Jack san? Did the priest do the right thing? Or should he have told the family about the letter?"

I thought about this sad woman. After she died, she didn't want her husband to know about the letter, because he would be upset.

"I think the priest did the right thing," I said.

6. THE LITTLE BROTHERS

Place: Tottori City, Tottori Prefecture

After we left Kyoto, we went back to Matsue for a few days. I enjoyed Kyoto, but it is a very big city, and I wanted to spend some time in Mr Yamada's peaceful hometown. One afternoon, we met one of Mr Yamada's neighbours. She was an elderly lady, about ninety years old. She didn't speak any English, but she was very friendly. She was from Tottori City. Mr Yamada told her I liked ghost stories. She said to Mr Yamada, 'You must tell him the story from Tottori about the little brothers!'

So, later, when we were watching the sun set over the big lake in the centre of Matsue, Mr Yamada told me the story.

"A long time ago, a man opened a small hotel in Tottori. He didn't have much money, so he bought everything at second-hand shops. The hotel rooms didn't have beds. They had traditional Japanese futons. He bought the futons at second-hand shops too. Everything was cheap and old, but it was all clean. The owner was very pleased.

"On the first night, a guest arrived. He enjoyed a nice meal and drank a lot of sake. He talked to the owner for a long time. Then, he looked at the clock. 'It's getting late, and I'm very tired. I think I'll go to my room now.' 'OK, good night. Sleep well,' said the owner.

"The guest went to his room and got into his futon. But after a few minutes, he could hear two children's voices. *Where are those children? They must be in the next room. But I can hear them clearly. Maybe they are in this room,* he thought. A child's voice said, 'Elder brother, are you cold?' And then another child's voice said, 'No, little brother. Are you cold?'

"The guest got up and looked around the room, but he couldn't see any children. He got back into his futon. But the voices continued. The guest started to feel very frightened. The voices were in his futon! So he ran downstairs and told the owner. 'There are children in my futon! I can hear voices from my futon!' The owner looked at him. 'You are having a bad dream! There is nothing in the futon! And you drank a lot of sake…' The guest became angry. 'I cannot stay here. I'm going!' And the guest left the hotel.

"The next night, another guest came and stayed in that room. He also heard the voices in the futon! But he had not drunk any sake. The owner became very angry. *Someone is trying to destroy my business!* he thought. *I will stay in that room tonight. I will use that futon! There is nothing in that futon! These people are crazy!*

"So the owner got into the futon, and turned off the light. Then, he heard two voices, 'Elder brother, are you cold?' 'No, little brother. Are you cold?' The two voices repeated the same questions. The owner became very frightened. The voices were coming from the futon. *It was true!* he thought.

"So, the next day, the owner took the futon back to the second-hand shop, and asked the shop owner about it. The shop owner said, 'I bought the futon from a smaller shop. You should go there. I can't help you.' So, the hotel owner went to that shop, and he heard this story.

"A very poor family owned the futon. The father of the house died, and the mother and her two children were alone. The boys were six and eight years old. Their mother worked very hard, but they were very poor and didn't have much food. They had no money to pay the rent, so the landlord was always very angry. He went to the house every day and asked for his money. The mother became very sick and soon died. So the boys were alone. They started to sell the things in their house, so they could pay the rent to the angry landlord. Soon, they only had the futon left.

"Winter came, and they had no money. They stayed together in the futon, and tried to keep warm. The younger child said, 'Elder brother, are you cold?' And the older brother said, 'No, little brother. Are you cold?'

"The landlord came to the house at night. He said to the two young boys, 'Where is my money? Where is my rent? You can't pay me? Well, get out!' So the boys had to leave the house. It was a cold, snowy night. The landlord looked around the house. *Can I sell anything?* he thought. The house was empty. There was only the futon left. *Ah! I can sell this futon! I can sell it to the second-hand shop.*

"The boys had no family, and they were alone, and homeless. The older brother said, 'There is a temple of Kannon near here. Let's walk to the temple. The priest at the temple will help us.' 'But the snow is very heavy, and it is very windy. Let's wait until tomorrow,' said the younger brother. 'We can't walk to the temple in this weather.'

"So they went back to the house. They tried to get into the house, but the door and windows were locked. They hugged each other, and sat down next to the house, and tried to keep warm. They became cold and sleepy, and soon, a blanket of snow covered them. A few days later, someone found the boys. They were dead. The priest buried them in the graveyard of the temple of Kannon.

"After the hotel owner heard this story, he took the futon to the temple of Kannon. He told the priests the story of the futon and asked them to pray for the little boys. So, the priests of the temple prayed over the futon, and the children found peace. The futon never spoke again."

After Mr Yamada told his story, we were quiet for a few minutes. It was a very sad story. The sun had set, and it was starting to get cold.

"Come on Old Jack san. Let's go back. We need a cup of nice warm sake," said Mr Yamada.

"That was a very sad story. I think a cup of warm sake is a good idea," I said.

That night, I lay in my futon in my room at Mr Yamada's house. I liked sleeping in the futon. It was very comfortable. But I thought about the two young boys in the story. They had a very sad life.

I spent a few more days in Matsue, and then it was time to say goodbye to Mr and Mrs Yamada, and to Japan. I had a wonderful trip, and a great experience. I will never forget it. And I heard some wonderful stories too. I will remember them for the rest of my life.

THANK YOU

Thank you for reading Old Jack's Ghost Stories from Japan. (Word count: 6,680) Old Jack hopes you enjoyed reading his stories.

For more information about the places in this book, please visit http://www.italk-youtalk.com. There is a page with maps and photographs of the places that Old Jack has written about.

If you would like to read more graded readers, please visit our website http://www.italkyoutalk.com

Other graded readers by Old Jack:
Old Jack's Ghost Stories from England (1)
Old Jack's Ghost Stories from England (2)
Old Jack's Ghost Stories from Scotland
Old Jack's Ghost Stories from Wales
Old Jack's Ghost Stories from Ireland

NOTES AND REFERENCES

1. A Mother's Love
From The Chief City of the Province of the Gods, Project
Gutenberg's Glimpses of Unfamiliar Japan, by Lafcadio Hearn (First
Series)
http://www.gutenberg.org/files/8130/8130.txt (Retrieved March,
2015)

2. The Laughing Samurai
From The Chief City of the Province of the Gods, Project
Gutenberg's Glimpses of Unfamiliar Japan, by Lafcadio Hearn (First
Series)
http://www.gutenberg.org/files/8130/8130.txt (Retrieved March,
2015)

3. The Blind Man Who Could See
Original story title: The Story of Mimi-Nashi-Hoichi
From The Project Gutenberg EBook of Kwaidan: Stories and Studies
of Strange
Things, by Lafcadio Hearn
http://www.gutenberg.org/files/1210/1210.txt (Retrieved March,
2015)

4. The Woman of the Snow
Original story title: Yuki-Onna
From The Project Gutenberg EBook of Kwaidan: Stories and Studies

of Strange
Things, by Lafcadio Hearn
http://www.gutenberg.org/files/1210/1210.txt (Retrieved March, 2015)

5. Secrets of the Heart
Original story title: A Dead Secret
From The Project Gutenberg EBook of Kwaidan: Stories and Studies
of Strange
Things, by Lafcadio Hearn
http://www.gutenberg.org/files/1210/1210.txt (Retrieved March, 2015)

6. The Little Brothers
From By the Japanese Sea, Project Gutenberg's Glimpses of
Unfamiliar Japan, by Lafcadio Hearn (Second Series)
http://www.gutenberg.org/files/8133/8133.txt

ABOUT THE AUTHOR

I Talk You Talk Press is a Japan-based publisher of language textbooks, graded readers and language learning/teaching resources.

Our team is made up of highly experienced language teachers and translators, who have all studied at least one additional language to an advanced level.

This experience enables us to design our materials from the perspective of both the teacher and the learner. We consult with both teachers and language learners when designing our textbooks and graded readers, and test our materials extensively in the classroom before publication.

We are a fast-growing press, and currently publish graded readers for learners of English. We publish new graded readers monthly.

www.ingramcontent.com/pod-product-compliance
Lightning Source LLC
Chambersburg PA
CBHW022350040426
42449CB00006B/814